TO THAT MYTHIC COUNTRY
CALLED CLOSURE

TO THAT MYTHIC COUNTRY CALLED CLOSURE

M

CONCRETE WOLF
POETRY CHAPBOOK SERIES

ISBN 978-0-9797137-7-4

Design by Tonya Namura
using Perpetua

Cover art: iStockphoto/Thinkstock

Author photo: Miles Gentry

Concrete Wolf Poetry Chapbook Series

Concrete Wolf
PO Box 1808
Kingston, WA 98346

ConcreteWolf.com

ConcreteWolf@yahoo.com

Most people were moving on . . . but there were fifteen odd families, where the spouse, I think it was probably all women, they just kept crying and crying. It's not my business to say that to a woman, "Suck it up and get going," but that is the way I feel. You've got to look to the future.

—Michael Bloomberg, in recalling his experience at the World Trade Center in 2002 to judges who were selecting the memorial, from *Green-Wood* by Allison Cobb (Factory School, 2010)

Acknowledgements

(in alphabetical order by poem title):

"Birds as omens for a change" (prior version):
Poems Niederngasse, October 2000

"Complaint to Lucy's shoe, found in a bowl of popcorn at 8:00 a.m." (prior version): *Pedestal, Issue 30, 2005*

"Conceding to Catholicism" (prior version):
Stirring: A Literary Collection, August 2000

"For those who never know what to say …": *Rattle, Winter 2012, Issue #38 / Finalist, Rattle 2012 Poetry Prize*

"Getting up on the wrong side of the dead" (prior version):
Mannequin Envy, December 2007

"In 80 days": *The Salt River Review, Spring 2009*

"New Jersey Bill and the China Doll play blackjack": *The Dirty Napkin, Fall 2008, V:1.4*

"Salt": *Rattle, Winter 2009, Issue #32*

"Shoes brought me to this place" (prior version):
Half-Drunk Muse, Spring 2006

"This is a poem not about Christmas": *OSPA Spring 2008 Contest, Third Place*

"To a husband, saved by death at 48": *Rattle, Winter 2011, Issue #36 / 2nd Place Finalist, Rattle 2011 Poetry Prize*

"Two women in the garden of the ward": *three candles*

"What widows know": *Mannequin Envy, December 2007*

"When one door closes" (prior version): *Half-Drunk Muse, Spring 2006*

"While my mother rots in Memory Care at Regency Park": *Rattle, Winter 2010, Issue #34*

"Yes, we the young widows": *Finalist, 2013 Split This Rock Poetry Contest*

Table of Contents

To That Mythic Country Called Closure

Yes, we the young widows

take Ambien to sleep, Ativan for anxiety,
Celexa just to scrape off the haze.
We fear barbecue grills, give his motorcycle
to his best friend. We wear wedding bands
too large for thumbs, make a bathroom fixture
of his dirty coffee mug, buy towels
to match. We sit in his chair,
stare at our own vacant one. Any man
on a motorcycle makes us wish
we'd kept our helmets.
We'd never tell you we performed
CPR while he vomited in our mouths.
And that we'd do it again.
What would erase that taste?

We hate your sad eyes, your Teleflora
delivery vans, cards telling us
our "insert Name of Deceased"
will remain forever in your hearts
where they don't belong. Please don't send
God's love to enfold us. We hate God.
We'd hate God less if,
while he was snatching our husbands,
he'd had the courtesy to set the garage
on fire. We hate having to comfort
you when you call. Hate you simply
because we once were you, convinced
we were prepared.

For those who never
know what to say to widows

Two months after the funeral, leave your wife and two
teenage sons, drive fourteen hours straight from Eagle to
walk up our porch unannounced. Open the garage door
the way people used to. The remote is broken. Fix it.
Take four truckloads of scrap lumber, crumbling drywall,
and junk appliances to the dump. Cook a chili so fine
we forget our lost appetites. Open a bottle of anything
that costs less than a sympathy card. Lie behind us on
the futon. Touch us, because other than one 20-minute
appointment with a gynecologist's plastic speculum,
we've gone from being touched all the time to being held
as if we'd spent half a hot day cleaning Cutthroats from
Gore Creek. Tell us that story. Again. The one where you
and Nick drop acid and drive his flat-black Valiant with no
dashboard to Wyoming to hunt jackalope. In a blizzard.
About getting to milk one because the females sleep
belly up. Say, *No, honest*. Waking up in the Casper rescue
mission wearing other people's clothes. Say, *Hey, it was
monomyth, babe*. Sleep in the guest room. After breakfast,
tie down Nick's '74 Suzuki in your truckbed with red
ratchet straps, slap the seat, once she's secure. Say, *He was
an original*. Kiss us like you mean something, even though
you don't know what the hell that is. Maybe it's just three
decades of Nick, and we're the last thing that touched
him. Take I-80 east. Manage to keep your shit together
until Elko, at least.

New Jersey Bill and the
China Doll play blackjack

It would be obvious to a guy with only one eye
that I don't belong here. I lose Nick to the couple
watching a made-for-TV movie and arguing the tenor
of Charlie Manson's insanity (he says simple schizophrenia,
she says schizophrenia with paranoid tendencies)
while they burn powder to liquid
in a silver spoon. Talk to Alan, they tell Nick.
Alan deals because he has kids
in college like everybody else who lives in this cardboard
complex whose suburban façade fools
no one. In the kitchen I find the only guy with a straw
in his Coca Cola. He stares long
and says *Did anybody ever say*
you look like a china doll? Sit down. You play cards?
Not well enough to bet my 401K. He flips cards
like flapjacks and pushes a pile of pretzel sticks
to my side of the table. I throw back two sticks.
He throws in four.

New Jersey Bill has eyes that have seen men bounce
like pinballs in the alley behind the R & R Bar,
and hands that held his wife's head out of the gutter water,
the wife who took him two bad marriages to find.
That night it rained too much Jack Daniel's,
the only night he drove Auburn Road with his seatbelt on
and she didn't. He asks
What are you supposed to do about that, doll?
and points to the space in his chest
where his life used to be. He smiles

like a congressman who spends his kids' quality time
riding trains from Trenton to Washington.
He's not talking about the eight years
vehicular manslaughter gave him
in a living room with a toilet,
and he doesn't try to pretend
it's the light bulb over his head making his eyes water.
He starts singing *Heart and soul, I fell in love with you,*
heart and soul, the way a fool would do, madly.
I told Nick *No* ten years ago. I predicted everything
we owned would go straight up his nose.
We married madly anyway
and diabetes stole it all instead.
You're asking the wrong doll, New Jersey.
Remember when smoke was smoke?
When weed was art, not medicine.
And pretzels had the decency not to stare
back at you from the bottom of a bowl.
This is when that one-eyed jack
who rarely hangs out with the perfect ten
show up together on my side of the table.
Bill is shifting like a small inside an extra large T-shirt,
his head bobbing in rhythm to the dog he had
on the back dash of the car.
Shit, New Jersey, tell me——
what are *you* going to do about that?

Birds as omens for a change

April 22: we sputter outside a MiniMart
in my sister's planned community near Baltimore.
Inside, you argue with the Pakistani owner
over hot dogs, maps. Maybe you were Hart Crane
in a former life. How you'll decide
to end this one is questionable. The motor

is running; quick escapes are your M.O.
Simon and Garfunkel kick around
the radio; a fabricated pond, too many
trumped up trees stand on my right-hand side.
Hire Rasputin to direct set design
and this is what you get. I am looking

up. Two western grebes soar,
swoop, dive, shampoo, rinse, repeat
around the pond.
They are off-course. Six years

ago precisely, a wasted merlin,
not aquatic, veered, dived;
ill-timed syncopation. A bridge, troubled water
laid him down. I bowed my head
to that alliance, kept it low
through the interment
and years of sidewalks
where the only change I bummed
was made of mercury or wood.

The grebes hesitate, flick wings,
run on water more miraculously

than a god who merely walked,
completely immerse, then lift.
With head bowed, I would have
missed this. You return to our car.
I look you straight in the eye.

Conceding to Catholicism

I include your electric razor
in a satchel packed with socks and underwear—
principled provisions; I detest butternut,
but I wear that dress because you like it.

They confiscate the razor, against the rules.
You'll run amok,
shave yourself to death.
Comedy sneers at fear—my heart beats.

I am deaf to a man who strokes
my head, snares my unwashed hair.
Go blind to a woman in gray, waiting
for waylaid, unsuspecting buses.

They unlock your door; you lie
unbalanced on the floor, reading
magazines upside down through
frames whose lenses came unglued.

You smile—good breeding,
not remembrance. Soon we're eating ice
cream, civilize an afternoon, from paper-tiger
cups to harmless wooden spoons.

Sensing my heart slow, you play piano
on your dresser, though you've had no lessons;
instruments here sing paroxysm,
not harmonies. You ask my name again.

You entreat me not to leave you
in this imbroglio, profess your Cheerios
are poisoned, confide Mata Hari fried
for less than you have leaked to me.

You speak secret German spy code,
maintain your monkey is a mole; madness
as abstraction was unsociable. Now,
its sour head is lying in my lap.

It abducts you and our biography
with it too; pulls my plugs,
plugs my throat, very nearly halts
the measures of my heart.

Doctors call it "stone heart"—
one so frozen with fear
or shock that it forgets to beat.

Later, I light candles, convert
our bedroom to a church; turn
to a rosary like a malcontent
novitiate turned nun.

The bead between *Hail Mary*
and *Our Father* pleads for stone
heart to take me, for fear or shock
to kill me sometime in the night.

When one door closes

The door is round and open. Don't go back to sleep.
Rumi

Nick is naked when they storm the door.
I struggle to cover him. They've brought
the sheet—white cotton, meager
thread count, standard size for beds
and bodies. I sew a sail of that cloth
with the needles he left behind.
Set him to sea like a chieftain on a boat,
my sister says. I tell her ships won't sink
on city streets. I give him to strangers instead,
transfixed until the van's metal doors slam shut.

I am the metallic sound of a failed provider, leaving him
in the cold with the thinnest fabric, no coin
in his mouth. The entry to our home remains
ajar for days, a broken yew strewn across
the threshold. When that passageway closes,
I tell Francesca I am the traitor who deadbolts
the door against a husband unfaithful
enough to die. *What else is there to do*
when it's cold outside? she asks. In my hand
is his band of gold, their archeological find.
I swallow the ring, a proper reburial,
and in my stomach it spins
round, full, open.

Communing with the deceased

Tell me something. What good could have come
from this? I'm prone in a wildflower field
in Eagle, Colorado. I have bourbon
in my glass and I don't drink. I feel queasy.

There is a gathering of people behind me
under a rented canopy, the white ones used for weddings
and times like these. All of them knew you better
than they know me. They carry canapés in their hands,

stories of your exploits on their lips, undigested grief
in that tender spot below the breastbone.
I'm clawing at the knapweed and they pretend
there's nothing wrong with that.

What can I tell our daughter about her late father
that she doesn't already know? That a blackball
in the bloodstream is as inheritable as my fear of water,
your love of Escher's delusions, our combined faith

that gravity's opposite is comedy? That we ignored the risks
of genetic disease, birthed her anyway? What good would
have come of another? Better to know we loved her well
enough to leave well enough alone. Do what we had to do.

It is mid June. The lupine are late to bloom this high
in the hills and there is no son who requires an explanation
of love and death. Nor to lose again to them. No stranger
at a wake need lead him away from a mother who lies

in the dirt. All this is easier without him than with him. It is, isn't it? Speak to me.

Shoes brought me to this place

I thought people shuffled quietly
in places like this. No, they march.
At 2:00 a.m. Sometimes
nude. Bare feet can make good boots.
Though what you've heard
about the screaming
is true.

I slip through rooms in black felt clogs
many sizes too large and *n/um tchai*
until dawn. They force me to breakfast
with the others, tell me to eat eggs if I wish
to be whole. *Scrambled is good for me?*
Scrambled was the van
that carried me here. My fork shakes
like the shekere I bought from a Nigerian man
who whistled through his harelip
and taught me how to dance.

The woman who eats my eggs
draws balloons on my breakfast tray.
The reason you can't fly is you're too attached
to artifacts. I tell her it's the pull
of shoes. She says we're all addicted
to something. I sketch sandals
on her bare feet. She turns into someone
else's conclusions, rises like a hallelujah,
flees for the open window.
The sweaty man across the table says there are
no balloons, eyebrows crawling up his forehead
like caterpillars to cocoon in his hairline.

He has some authority here.
He wants my shoes. I tell him they are not mine
to give. He kneels at my feet
to remove them. I bite the sunburn
on the back of his neck. I eat, sleep, bathe
in shoes. When the shrieking starts
late at night, I hide inside them, soft
and safe. They are risk, ritual, reward.
He is dead, the therapist tells me.
No, not if his shoes still dance.

To the One I've Hurt
(letter to Nick I'll burn on
a borrowed barbecue next Friday)

Would you think it ironic I've landed where I once
committed you? This city holds no other rehab for widows
strung out on grief, who refuse food and sleep as if they
were poison, who lie on highways counting on a Peterbilt
with a driver blind from an 18-hour run, new Hondas
stacked like cord wood for the dealership on Kietzke Lane.

We discuss degrees of damage when we're escorted to
picnic tables protected by a canvas awning, though we'd
prefer the rain. Dan, of Early Times in earlier times.
Howie, chief of cooked spoons and unwashed syringes.
Jane, mistress of Zig-Zag and double-wide spliffs. The
counselor hands out Marlboros and Winstons from a bowl,
last names written large in black marker on cellophane
as see-through as our resolution. We pass around the one
Zippo twelve of us are allowed, and pray six hours till the
next smoke pass quickly.

They believe I'm special, but we're all just uncontrollables
no one on the outside wants to deal with anymore. Our
security blankets shredded. Walking proof for at least three
of the five stages of grief. You know how people hate it
when you cry.

This will make you laugh. *Hey, I can teach you to shoot some
hoops*, Howie said. I've never even held a basketball. But
here we are on the court playing H-O-R-S-E. Howie,
a thoroughbred on blacktop; me, scheduled for the

slaughterhouse. We've been shooting for over an hour, repetitive the way we like things. When we hear that clang off the iron that gives him an E, he hugs me. *Sorry about that, man. Didn't mean to, like, maul you or anything.* Hey, Howie, it doesn't count if you take a fall short of the finish.

I'm to attend daily group sessions Jane has nicknamed *You're Not the Only One You're Killing*, and *Love Is the Many Ways We'll Make You Keep Saying You're Sorry*, though my only addiction is a dead man. Unmonitored is unthinkable, so I do as I'm told. I pace out dimensions. Constant movement is my handicap. Eighteen indoor/outdoor carpet tiles from the windows to the door, perfect match for the Armstrong suspended squares. There's a fork stuck in the ceiling. Popular game here once. Throw silver at heaven when no one's watching. If it sticks, you're done. People whose job it is to cure us figured it out when a fork dropped like a miracle on the therapist who needed one for his baked beans. Now it's plastic only.

Dan tells me visiting therapists are the worst—*No time to make friends with our eccentricities.* This one has clipped blonde hair and a pencil skirt that looks pained, stretched across her thighs. *Excuse me—you in the back. If you can't sit down, you'll have to leave.* "I'm sorry," I say, "if I sit, I die." No one moves but me. I hear *Go. Now.* A chair scrapes. I hear *If she leaves, I leave.* Howie. Then Jane. Dan. Nine unbroken horses. Only two settle in their stalls.

Two women in the garden of the ward

*I had a farm in Africa, at the foot of the Ngong Hills . . . In the
day-time, you felt that you had got high up, near to the sun, but
the early mornings and evenings were limpid and restful, and the
nights were cold.*

Isak Dinesen, "Out of Africa"

On restful mornings, Emma and I tie crimson bandannas
around our heads. We are told the florid color will make
our movement through the garden easier to track. For
security we must share a single pair of pruning shears.
Only the red-headed woodpeckers who nest in dead
trees accept us as their own. Old growth branches of the
butterfly bushes need heavy pruning, but Emma's hands
are clumsy and her clippings modest. The tranquilizer
she's been given has left her tentative. Each cut, the nurses
assure, will move her nearer to the sun.

She does not speak ill of anyone but herself. I read to her
of Blixen's farm, slightly bitter scents of coffee-blossoms.
She asks if she might smell the pages as though perfumes
could linger there. Emma is loved by someone poor and
must leave this place when the money runs out.

One limpid evening, I knot the end of my bandanna on
the branch of a sawtooth oak; I imagine the fabric hangs
like the newspapers say Emma did in the cold of the night.
I hack so far into the heartwood, I know the butterfly
bushes will not live. A legion of woodpeckers ascend, bow
their red heads in deference to me on their passage to

more hospitable climes. I have cut with so much passion the pruning shears are split in two, yet I find myself no nearer to the sun.

In this room down a hall
at the Hopewell House
every Wednesday
from 6:30 to 8:00 p.m.,
the widowed have agreed to meet
to lick the salt block.
My name tag reads
Albino deer (recessive rarity): widow at 42.
Dun-colored Helen and Marie
mistake me for a sheep or a goat
as we draw our chairs into a circle
of circumstance. Muscles in their aged faces
twitch with the greed of suspicion.
In the larger world,
Jean and I would sit in adjoining streetcar seats,
read our newspapers,
and never share a headline.
Even Doris, who drags the remains of a personal god
at the bottom of her purse,
tucked next to non-prescription reading glasses
she bought on sale at Walmart,
shrinks from my pink eyes.
Louise has ten grandchildren,
three she and Harry were raising
because her daughter is, well, you know,
she doesn't want to say. She won't tell you either
that when Harry up and died like that,
some small part of her wished
he'd had the decency to take those kids with him,
but he never even took them to the park.

Betty lost a husband and found
a lump. Elsie says when the ambulance comes
to the Ridgewood Nursing Home,
they don't turn on the siren
for fear they'll incite a riot
of dying. Ida says *yeah*, she knows.
She's lost two of them that way. I nod.
Judith's raised eyebrow asks
What could one with hooves so pale know of loss?
A marriage must be long
to be 40-years deep,
and grief is a black market business
best kept to themselves. If I taste it,
others will want it.
Young bucks will be dying in droves.
In war, in the streets,
in flaming buildings.
Or quietly in a bed next to me at night.
That sting in the wound, that particular tang
on the tongue, are theirs.

Keep me away from the salt.
Their old ones are sanctified,
their sorrow is sacred,
denial alive in the hide.

Complaint to Lucy's shoe, found in a bowl of popcorn at 8:00 a.m.

This is new. Yesterday you camped
in the refrigerator, the morning
before, you slithered under the toy box
like a Coral snake making Lucy late
and me crazy. You hang on too long
after the bite.

You and her Chatty Kathy doll
are in cahoots. You yank Chatty's cord.
She jabbers at me about schoolmates
and Barbie dolls, ballet classes
and SpongeBob SquarePants.

Your grommets remind me of ties
that bind—shoelaces, clinging vines,
apron strings. Another mother somewhere outside
Baltimore glides into her children's room at night,
suspires for the rise and fall of small chests
like billowed sails on Chesapeake Bay.
They breathe, she breathes easier.

I slump in the kitchen, swallow another slice
of birthday cake, use one of the tiny candles
to stab holes in Lucy's uneaten lasagna.
How do you feel when you're on
the wrong feet? You stick out your tongue;
I mash you into the frosting.

Outside the window, the postman places
a letter in our box, reconsiders, removes it.
Wrong address, recipient moved, change
of heart. Some awry deliveries rectified,
some scribbled in indelible ink.

Lucy would say my finger is poking my brain
in the eye and my teeth are chewing
my stomach. But my daughter is eight, and knows nothing
about how sleep stands in a corner
of the bedroom thumbing its nose at me.
Lucy can sleep on a staircase, head on the top step,
hip on the next, feet on the tread below that,
strung like a ribbon of placidity.
I go to the kitchen, spread pages of yesterday's
newspaper in a crossword puzzle on the table,
and make Easter eggs for her from balloons
wound with thin string dipped in starch.
I hear my mother saying
All your lopsided creations are minchiata
when she means guilty of a supremely solemn
stupid act. Lucy believes mine's a heavenly hand.
And who am I to argue?

The string is Phileas Fogg on a journey
around the balloon, but with fewer obstacles
to steal its fortune. Only the cat worries it,
batting occasionally. Nick told me a plotline
depends on the things that go wrong.
I woke that morning in bed with him
dead, his shoulder pressing my arm,
deflated on a fistful of needles and pins.
Diabetes is a real trip not a destination,
he'd quip. What would he say about traveling
around a balloon at night
without some sort of breaking point?

Lucy appears from her room to crack the china plate
of darkness, the bounce-back ability
of rubber balls riding on a yellow blanket
that trails her like a duckling in love.

She climbs her usual chair like she scales
the backyard mulberry. She is sweaty,
her blood glucose is low, so we drink
orange juice together. The everyday accompaniment
of scrambled eggs and milk,
bacon and toast are too far away at two
in the morning. What would she have done
if she'd known the consequence
of following too closely in a father's footprints?
Perhaps fetuses who run away
from the womb too soon
are only saying no. Her lazy eye
wanders left as if half of her believes
I own the rights to infallibility.
She brings air to a shrunken balloon
with the smallest puffs of life.
There is starch in her hair and an impulse
to fix it. *Where does Phileas go next*,
Lucy wants to know. Minchiata, my child.
Balloons burst inside a dozen eggs
until all that remains is string.

You.   Her.

You are in your own bed with the TV on
when the Towers fall. This bed you've rarely left
in the last five months, a bed like those defective drains
in swimming pools that grip a piece of ass,
thigh, arm, and hold them there below
until the person they belong to
drowns. You are also in this bed in the aftermath,
eyes forced open, retinas assaulted by image after flickering
horror flick image, until your eyes rest
on her.   Her.   A widow like you,
holding up a picture of a husband for anyone
who will take the time to look; a picture alive, well,
blonde hair slicked into a perfection of place
by a plastic comb, every feature in horizontal order
except for a slightly crooked upward tilt of smile
in the left-hand corner of his mouth.
There's an entire country's worth
of width between you both, but still you want
to love her, this woman who has lost as you have lost,
whose only wars thus far have been delivered
via the History Channel. A woman who asks little,
who only wants his body back. But you don't love.
You hate.   Her.   Where was she
on the morning of April 2nd? Standing upright at her stove,
cracking two raw eggs with one small hand into an iron
frying pan, sunny-side up, TV off, blissfully oblivious
to you.   You.   That April morning in this bed,
attempting to beat the life back into the body
of your beloved with a fist folded in on itself, trying
mouth-to-mouth with whatever was left

after the screaming.   Alone,
with bodily proof that you'd failed.
No camera crews, no parties
of rescue, no picture to hold up to an audience
of millions. And you hate yourself now for hating her,
her naïveté of what's to come. You don't understand
this hate, nor know what to do with it, so you ball it up
like a shit-stained bed sheet turned to 200,000 tons
of steel, turned to 600,000 feet of glass,
turned to 425,000 cubic yards of concrete—
surely enough weight to break a 32" TV screen—
and you drag her by the neck
through the shattered. Take her into an embrace
of hate   anguish
          panic confusion   fear   the weeping.
And you take her picture from her,
love it as if it were your own.

Getting up on the wrong side of the dead

Even death couldn't keep you
from the Smoke N Head, returning after six months,
a carton of Triumph in a brown bag.
You are not the night we dressed to scare
that Halloween in Eagle. I wore a bile-colored gown
I'd struggled over under the lackadaisical eye
of Mrs. Litterelle's home economics class
for a prom Jimmy Middelmas' rolled cigarette sleeve
neglected to attend. My hair was teased so much
it should have been embarrassed.
You had black shoe polish sewer grates
circling your eyes and an executioner's hood.
You were growl and grumble. Those kids turned liquid,
dropped their pillowcase sacks. Started up that ugly cry,
little faces puckered like dried apple people.
Run, boy, run! You'd grab the bags and go after them
to return the booty. I followed, the green witch
they knew from horror flicks,
trailing her rabid raccoon familiar.
I only made it worse.

That's the look I'd trust, but you don't look.
You feel behind me, knees drawn
in the cleft of mine, left arm a velvet
rope across my waist, holding me
back from all that lives
under the bed. Your hand cools
my nipple in the unremarkable
way you palmed water from a trout stream
on the ranch, bringing its honor

to your mouth. The way we'd slept solid
for sixteen years. *Coccyx sounds erotic*,
riding a triangle of good intentions to the base
of a spine. I don't want to look
at the familiar or turn a corner
of the bedspread, you becoming fluid seeping
through a pillowcase. A letting go
of candy buttons on paper tapes,
the fright who sends you back to the black.
That dried apple ugly cry.
Didn't I always make it worse.

While my mother rots in
Memory Care at Regency Park

At the Waffle House, if you're facing some bitter truth,
we'll save you a window booth. And we will be waiting.
David Wilcox, "Waffle House"

My 75-year-old father calls for the second time today
to tell me what he really wanted
was for my mother to have gotten
off their flowered couch in 1985
and boarded that Boeing 727 with him
to the Big Island. I've clamped the phone
between my shoulder and my ear, and a rusty can opener
that should have been buried in a landfill years ago
to the top of a 29 oz. can of Hunt's Tomato Puree.
It's cutting the edge of the lid
into tiny shark's teeth. My thumb is bleeding.
He's gone on to volcanoes, lava flows,
and black diamonds spewed in the air.
The CD player clicks and suddenly David Wilcox
is illuminating the finer points of altered states
after the midnight hour while scraping eggs
and flour from the napkin dispenser at the *Waffle House*.
I grab a napkin and ask If a black diamond
had a favorite song, what would it be?
He says Hmmm. I don't know—*That Old Black Magic*,
I guess. I say Black diamonds, black magic—
who wouldn't have thought of that?
You're not very original.
He says How the hell should I know
what a black diamond's favorite song would be?
Anyway, black diamonds don't listen to music.

30

I say How do you know? He says They don't have ears.
I say Like that's necessary. You're practically deaf,
and you constantly complain about your upstairs
neighbor with the swollen prostate waking you up
all night every time he pads barefoot to the bathroom
to pee. You don't seem to have any trouble
hearing with no ears. He says Okay, wait a minute—
a black diamond's favorite song is Daddy's Little
Pain-in-the-Ass Girl. I say Hey, old man, you called me.
He says Not to talk about what kind of music
black diamonds listen to. I say Well, what *do* you want
to talk about? He says
She never wanted to go anywhere.
Now it's too late.
Something I can't have, I guess.
She's my wife he says. I say She's my mother.
He wants me to say losing someone to death
is a step up from losing someone to dementia.
That Mrs. De Luca's calico cat,
who had his broken tail amputated an inch at a time,
hurts worse than the three blind mice combined.
That if she'd had the decency to die instead,
his grief would take him on a once-in-a-lifetime trip
to that mythic country called closure.
But I don't lie to him. I never have.
Even when it's necessary. I say Join the crowd.
I say If my husband was still alive,
I'd put him on the phone to argue with you
while I wrestle this big game fish of a can to the deck.
Maybe he could go get me a Band-Aid too.

He says I'll call you tomorrow. Or maybe I'll come visit.
Do you need anything?
I say Yeah, a new can opener would be good.
He says What kind of music do they listen to?

To a husband, saved by death at 48

You will not see me, now
older than you are.
You will not watch my toenails
harden into turtle shells.
You will not complain about my face
creams costing more than most people
spend on groceries in a month.
Nor see me apply them to my hands
because no matter how young a woman's face looks,
it's always the back of her hands
that give her away.
You will never think of me as a suitable gift
for a toddler on Christmas,
shrunken to doll size, wrapped in skin
as thin as bargain paper. You will not be the one
to drive me home wet
from the Lloyd Center Mall
where restrooms are hidden away like exclusive resorts
down remote corridors.
You will not need to remind me
to take my umbrella when it's raining,
nor find my car keys
in the refrigerator next to the eggs I bought yesterday,
and we will not laugh about it.
You will not hear me struggling with nouns.
You will never be awakened late on Friday evening
by a ringing phone, wife gone from your bed,
Detective Copeland saying she was found asking people
to help her find her husband
at a Taco Bell on Burnside

that stays open from 5:00 a.m. to 5:00 a.m.
every day but Sunday.
Someone else will sit with me in the ER
on New Year's Eve
listening to an alcohol poisoned teenage boy
vomit in the next room while we wait for news
about the golf ball on my temple,
received for nothing more complicated
than slipping off a curb.
You will not see me without my teeth
or my gallbladder. Never need to learn
I've been sexually inappropriate with Paul
in The Pearl Memory Care Residence at Kruse Way
where I live apart from you for the first time in fifty years.
You will not be the one to close my eyes.

Husbands of widows have it easy,

particularly the dead one. He's out of it,
a man taken by one hell of a mistress
whose wife must accept the infidelity,
and that he's still hanging around the apartment
like drapery, swaying from a rod, filtering
the undertones, bringing his brand of shadowing
to everything that goes on there. Changing songs
on the CD player, so you're forced to stop
in the middle of private conversations to say,
See, see! It's like a sign. That song meant something to us.
Except now the us isn't you and him, but you
and this other guy, the new husband,
who's wandered innocently enough
into this whole interior redecorating mess,
who's just standing there, that cute cowlick
sprouting a question mark on his forehead,
holding the bedroom slippers his mother bought
him for Christmas in his hands, being bombarded
by this damn song you're all excited about
that he's never even heard before in his life.
Wondering what the fuck
this has got to do with him,
and are you ever going to stop making
references to the dead guy he never met,
but certainly hears way too much about.
Like that night back in '83 (before you met him)
tucked away in a house in the woods outside Rye, NY
that belonged to the son of Ludlow Smith
who was married to Kate Hepburn
before she became famous, a moonlit fog

of Roxy Music wafting over you
while you were making love to the dead guy
(before he died) on a deck built around a birch
that's stuck forever now in the middle
of those red cedar boards like a knife to the heart.
He's in no condition to be competing
against anything, really, he's just trying to put away
his slippers like you told him to
because if you trip on them one more time
in the dark, you're seriously considering
making some kind of draperies out of him too.
Which would only add more deepening of expression
to the room—that something shadowing something bright
beyond the doubling of the white light, you know,
that heaven thing.

What widows know

If you had not died right
in the middle of our marriage,
the man who now calls himself
husband and I would still have bumped
elbows in the Starbucks on 12th Avenue,
forced to share the only empty
table, skating confidences
in figure eights between us
like stir sticks in coffee cups.
I would have sipped the musk
of his collarbone through a paper straw,
ridden the rise of his hip
in the half-light of rainy
Thursday afternoons.
He would have known the cruelty
of the heft of my breast in his hand;
I, the running home, begging
your fingers to untangle
strands of copper lightning
from my hair, smelling
of ozone after a thunderstorm.
Like children drunk on our own
weightlessness, we three
would have climbed too high up,
too far out on the limb
of a different inevitability.
You say *Choose*. I uncurl
my fingers from the branch.

This is a poem not about Christmas

and begins with the will to organize. Your perseverance
will be stretched the span of a greeting card list. Those
you've forgotten never find their way home. Those you
remember are children concerned only with what's
beneath your wrappings. You'll say: *who has that kind
of time?* People will light candles for you and pray. A
card will come. You'll wind your pain at great lengths
around the banisters. Boughs will pull apart, needles will
poke you. You'll say: *I really need to rest.* Carolers on the
nightshift will rouse you hourly with bottles full of tidings
of comfort. You might throw a silver bell, miss them and
hit an angel. You'll push a button and a light will blink.
Someone will answer the call thirty minutes later. You will
think you are a wise man. You thought you were a camel
once, but that didn't work out either. You'll say: *I don't
know what He wants.* Under the mistletoe, there'll be only
yourself to kiss. Because someone dropped it, a ball will
fall. There will be a struggle with something that looks
like a tricycle missing several crucial parts. And a rally
for a green bean casserole, expected but uneaten. Family
will gather: *don't you think her asparagus look too thin; isn't
her eggnog pale?* A glass will spill. Your sister will argue
with your husband over seating arrangements. Someone
will fling a saucer out the window. And you? You'll be
forgotten behind the cranberries, your face in the pecan
pie one of them was kind enough to bring.

Before your eyes finally close, you'll say: *next time, maybe
travel, maybe Greece.*

About the Author

M was born on the East Coast of the U.S. She's an only child, so she never had to share the backseat of the car, or her parents, with anyone. She's visited 41 states, two foreign countries, and three island nations. She eats grape tomatoes from the carton while standing in front of an open refrigerator, and dark chocolate like the government's going to make it illegal any minute. When confronted with paperwork requesting her marital status, she checks all the boxes since she's been single, married, divorced, widowed, and in a domestic partnership at one time or another during her life, and she's not certain when you stop being any of them. She most envies those who can sing, draw, or play a musical instrument. She owns approximately 2,000 vinyl record albums and CDs, one white 2000 Volkswagen Beetle with a sunroof she intends to keep in perpetuity, and more books than Powell's. If there's any truth to reincarnation, she'd like to come back as an architect or a gynecologist. She does her own manicures weekly, and has been known to wear foundation, mascara, and lipstick while undergoing major surgery. This is her first chapbook, dedicated to the exemplary men in her life:

First…	Frank
Past…	Miles
Future…	Stephen

Also From *Concrete Wolf Poetry Chapbook Series*

Where Good Swimmers Drown
Susan Elbe

A Broken Escalator Still Isn't The Stairs
Chuck Carlise

Four of a Kind
Mark Neely

Black Box Theater as Abandoned Zoo
Dana Elkun

What Sound Does It Make
Erin Malone

Eastlake Cleaners When Quality & Price Count [*a romance*]
Janet Norman Knox

A Pilgrim's Guide To Chaos in the Heartland
Jessica Goodfellow

Special Two Chapbook Issue:
Put Your Sorry Side Out   &   *The Way Out West*
Lois Marie Harrod   J.R. Thelin

Squeezers
Alison Pelegrin

Such Short Supply
Michelle Brooks

The Tallahassee Letters
Ryan G. Van Cleave

The Grape Painter
Lou Suarez